EUPHONIUM B.C.

MAKING M
MATTER

BAND METHOD

BOOK I: BEGINNING BAND

FRANK TICHELI
AND
GREGORY B. RUDGERS

BOB MARGOLIS, EDITOR

This book belongs to:

Micah M F6 pas14

Name of ~~Euphoniumist~~ bass player

Dear Band Member:

Welcome to *Making Music Matter* and congratulations on your decision to learn to play an instrument! You are beginning a journey that promises many rewarding experiences. As you travel along this exciting path, the skills you will learn go beyond learning to play an instrument. You will learn how music can express what words alone cannot. You will experience a joy that only music can bring. You will enjoy the satisfaction of making music with others. So, practice hard, learn all you can about music—its power and its mysteries—and above all, have fun!

Frank Ticheli & Gregory B. Rudgers

ISBN 1-59913-188-9
Photography by Vincent Aiosa, Valleyview Photography, Newfield, New York
Music engraved by David Teas — Fingering diagrams created with the Music Ed Fingering Fonts

MANHATTAN BEACH MUSIC

Center the mouthpiece, with slightly more upper lip in mouthpiece — may vary slightly from player to player.

Cradle Euphonium with left arm. Sit up straight, feet flat on the floor...

Fingers naturally curved.

WHAT YOU SHOULD KNOW
BEFORE THE FIRST LESSON

1. Staff

Below is a five-line **Staff** containing a **Bass Clef**, a **Key Signature** and a **Time Signature**. There are two measures. Each **Measure** is separated from the next by a **Bar Line**, and a **Final Bar Line** is used to show the end of a composition.

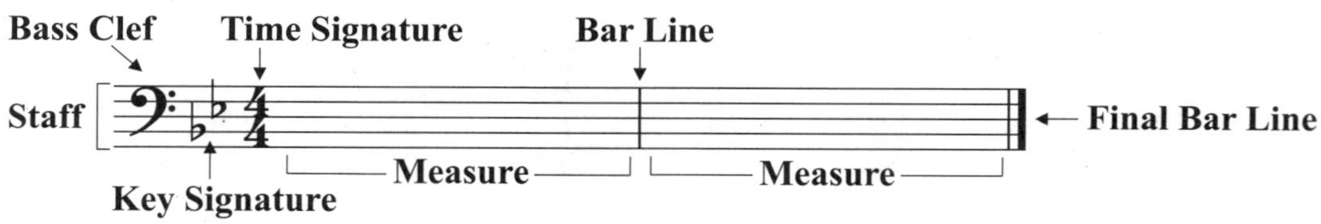

2. Whole Notes & Whole Rests - *each gets* 4 BEATS

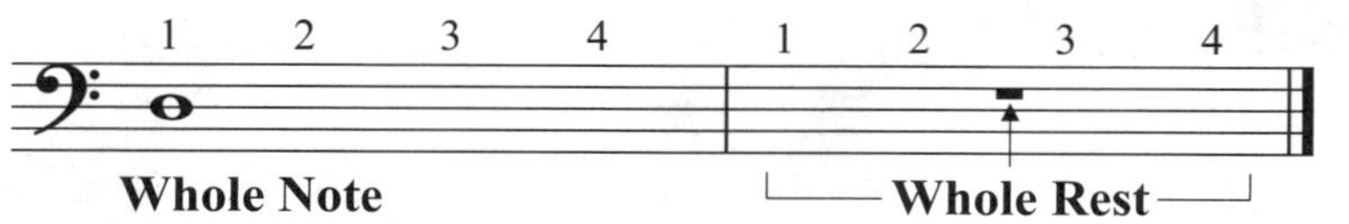

3. Half Notes & Half Rests *each gets* 2 BEATS

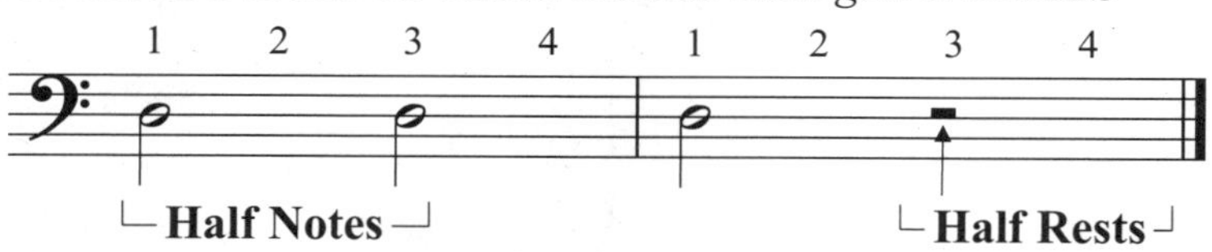

4. Quarter Notes & Quarter Rests *each gets* 1 BEAT

5. Flats & Sharps

6. Time Signatures

The Top Number = Number of BEATS in each **Measure**

The Bottom Number shows that the quarter note (shown as the number "4") gets 1 BEAT

Letter Names of the Pitches

NOTES and DATES TO REMEMBER

EUPHONIUM B.C.

GROUP 2

LESSON 1

EUPHONIUM FINGERINGS:
The valves are numbered 1, 2, and 3
(The No.1 valve is closest to the mouthpiece)
Valves in black should be **pressed down**.

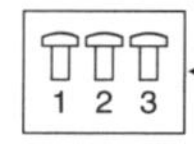

New in this lesson:

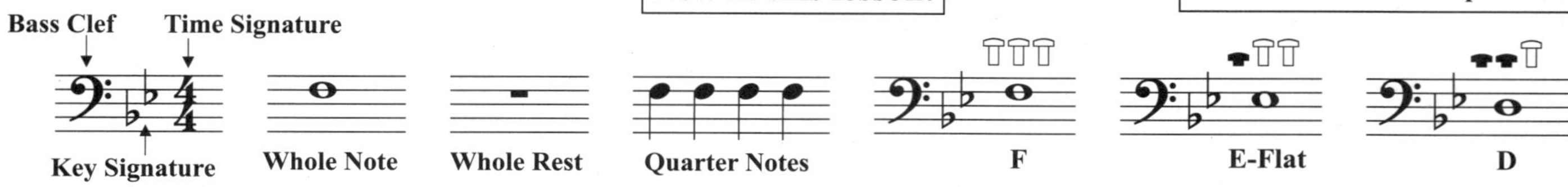

1 Whole Notes & Whole Rests

Count carefully and tap your foot on each beat.

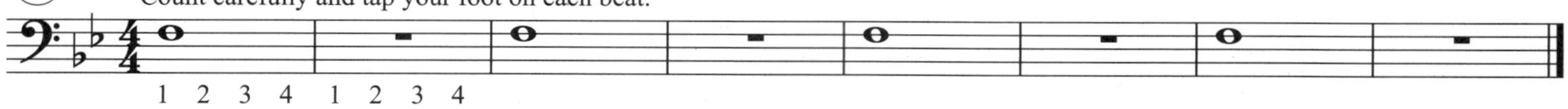

2 Quarter Notes

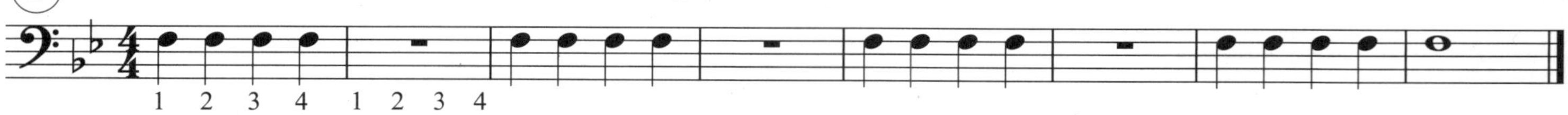

3

4

5

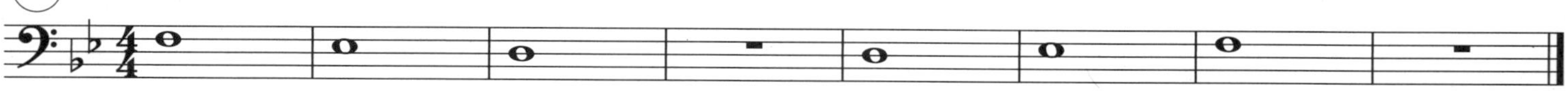

6

7 All Together Now

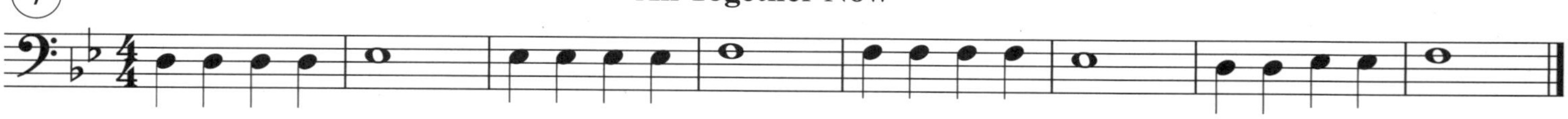

FIRST JOURNEY

COMPOSITION NO. 1

FRANK TICHELI

LESSON 2

New in this lesson:

Half Note Half Rest

Half Notes & Half Rests

1 Count carefully and tap your foot on each beat.

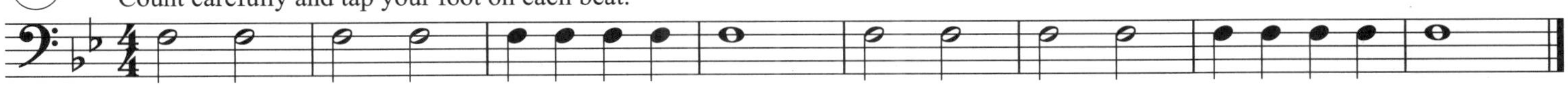

1 2 3 4

2

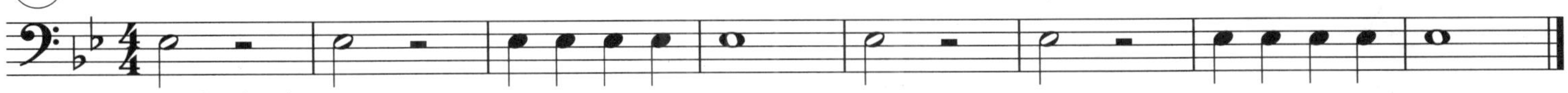

1 2 3 4

3

4

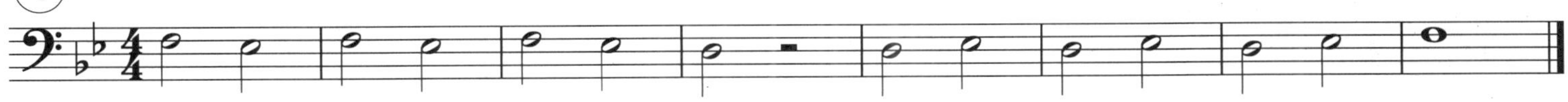

5

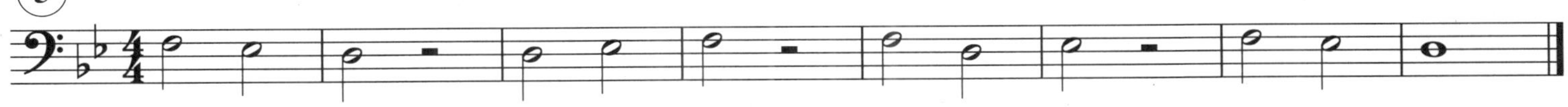

Stepping Down, Stepping Up

6

Old Man Kelsey

7

HER MAJESTY

COMPOSITION NO. 2

FRANK TICHELI

EUPHONIUM B.C.

GROUP 2

LESSON 3

New in this lesson:

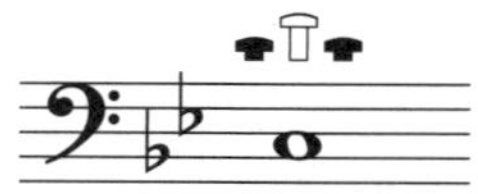

C

1

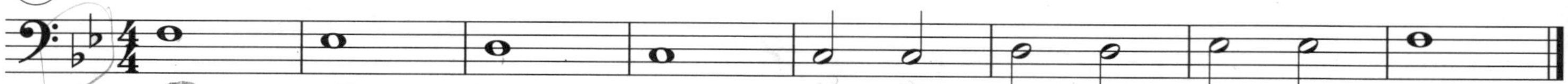

2

3 **Two Apiece**

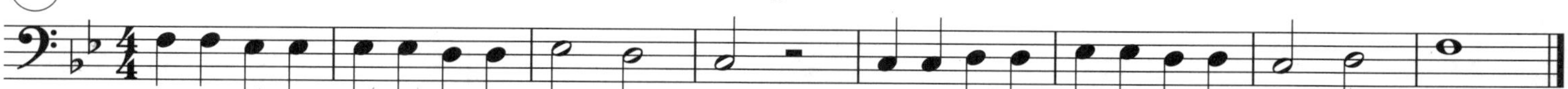

4 **Little Johnny, Little Mary**

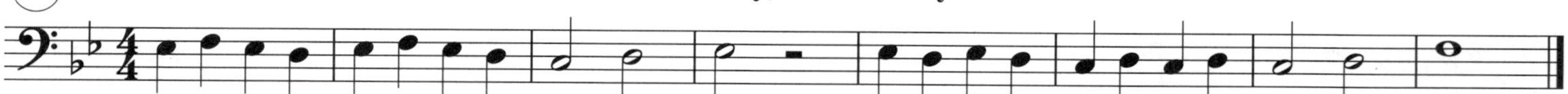

5

6 **Hello, Billy Joe**

7 **First Duet**

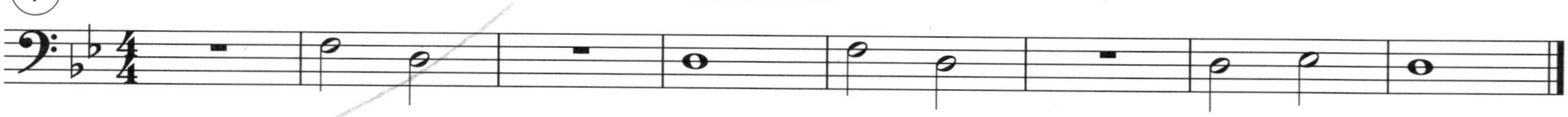

ANCIENT TREES

COMPOSITION NO. 3

FRANK TICHELI

LESSON 4

New in this lesson:

Two-Four Time Signature — Quarter Rest — B-flat — A

(1)

(2)

Quarter Rests

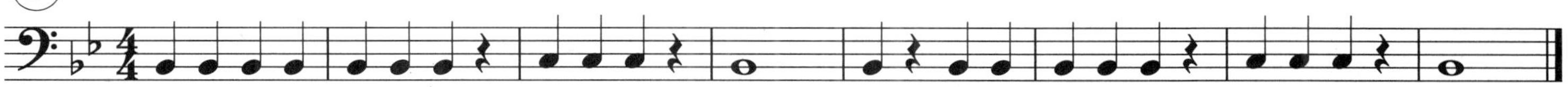

(3)

Two-Four Time

(4)

Good Old Baggy Bones

(5)

Leaping Down

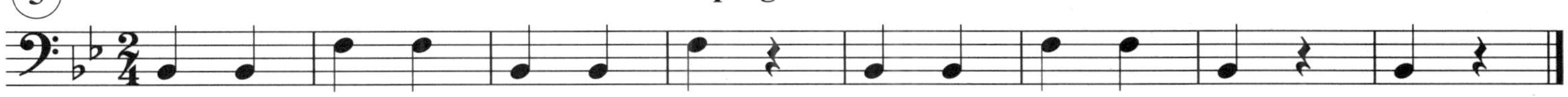

(6)

Trade Measure Duet

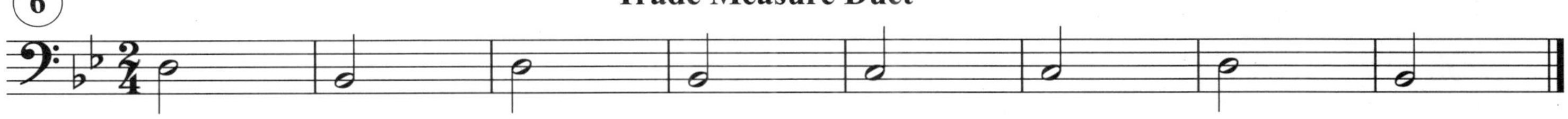

(7)

Four-Four Counting Test

HARVEST CELEBRATION

COMPOSITION NO. 4

FRANK TICHELI

EUPHONIUM B.C.

GROUP 2

LESSON 5

New in this lesson:

Three-Four Time Signature

Dotted Half Note

Tied Notes

1

Counting in Three

2

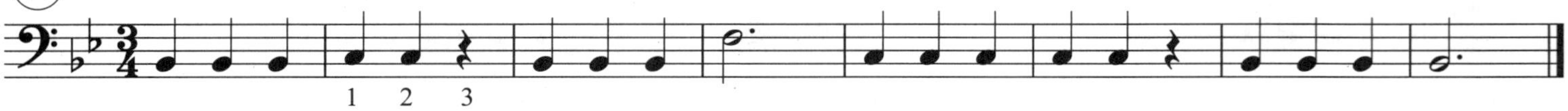

3

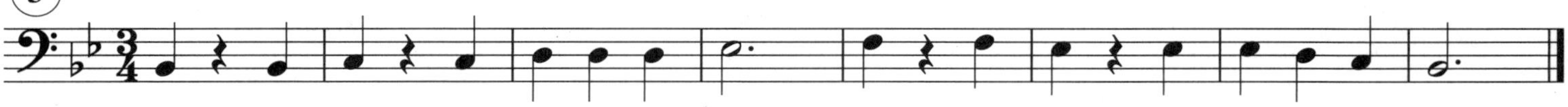

4

Half Quarter, Half Quarter

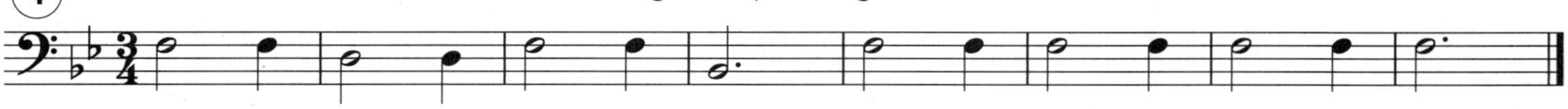

5

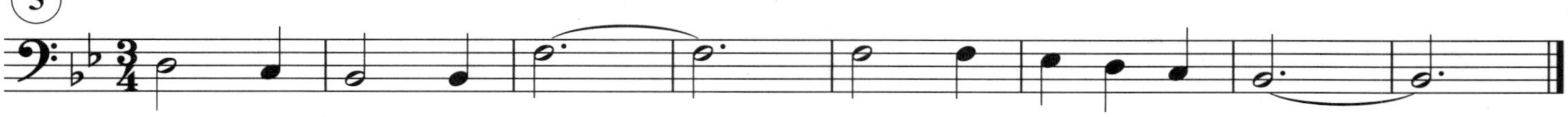

6

All Tied Up

7

Two-Four Ties

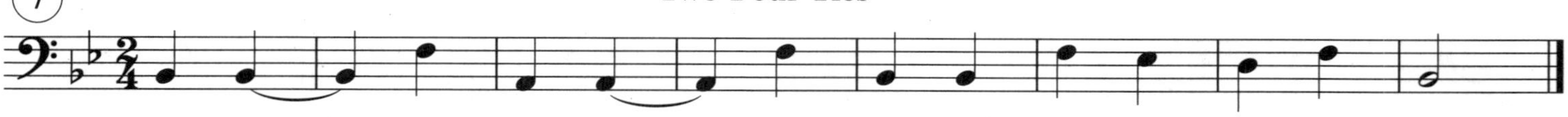

WALTZING IN THE RAIN

COMPOSITION NO. 5

FRANK TICHELI

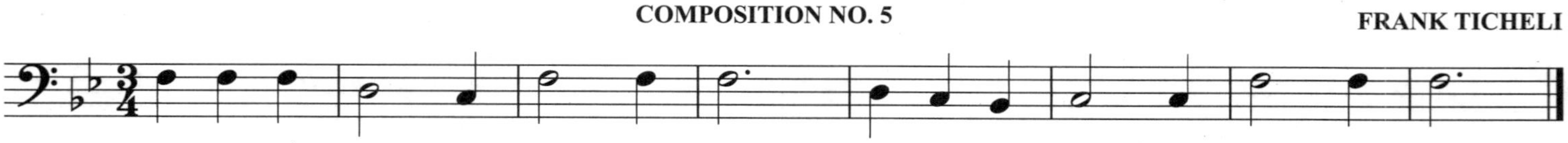

LESSON 6

New in this lesson:

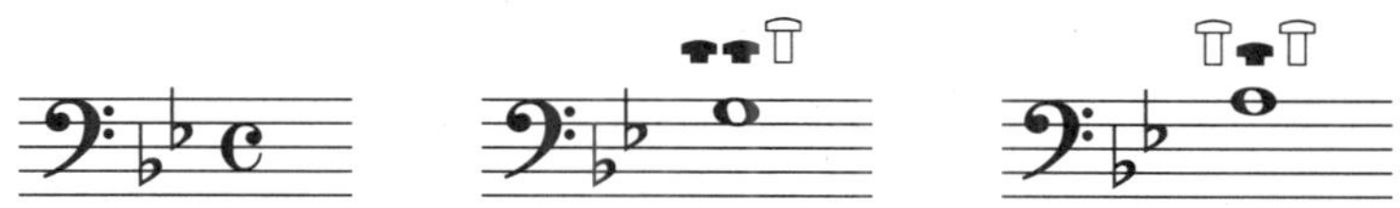

Common Time Signature | G | A

1

2

English Dance in Common Time

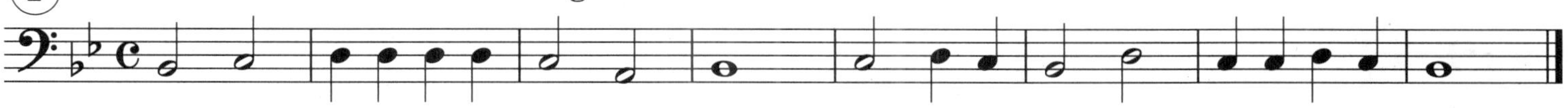

3

4

5

Oh, What A Day!

6

Oh, What A Perfect Day!

7

Taking Turns Duet

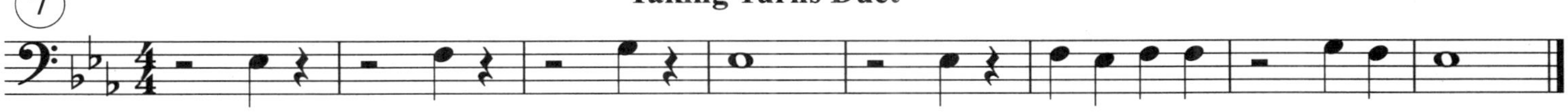

WALTZING IN THE SUNSHINE

COMPOSITION NO. 6

FRANK TICHELI

LESSON 7

New in this lesson:

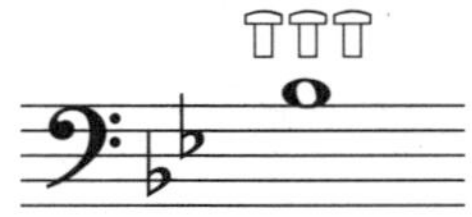

B-Flat

1

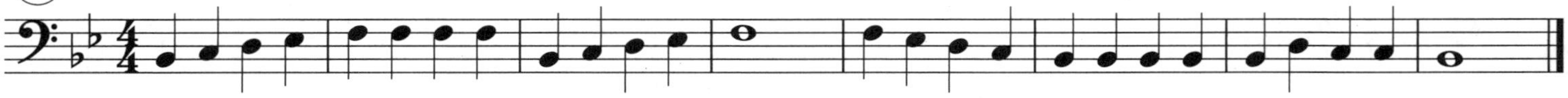

2

3

4

A Familiar Tune

5

Long Haul Truckers

DANCE OF THE JACK O'LANTERN

COMPOSITION NO. 7

FRANK TICHELI

LESSON 8

New in this lesson:

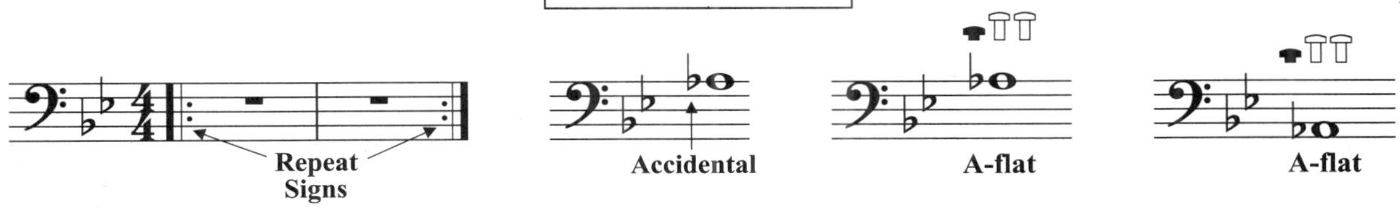

1

Accidentals

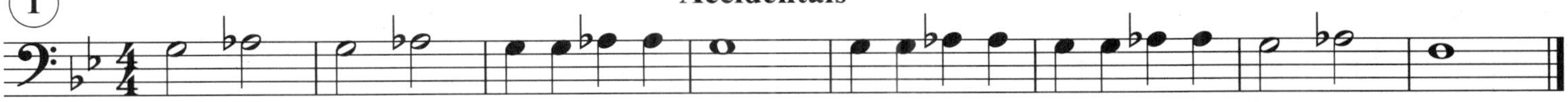

2

3

4

Red Light, Green Light

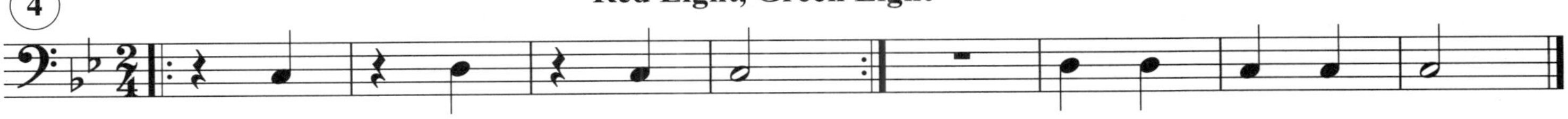

5

Waltz For Grandmas

A RENAISSANCE FAIR

COMPOSITION NO. 8

FRANK TICHELI

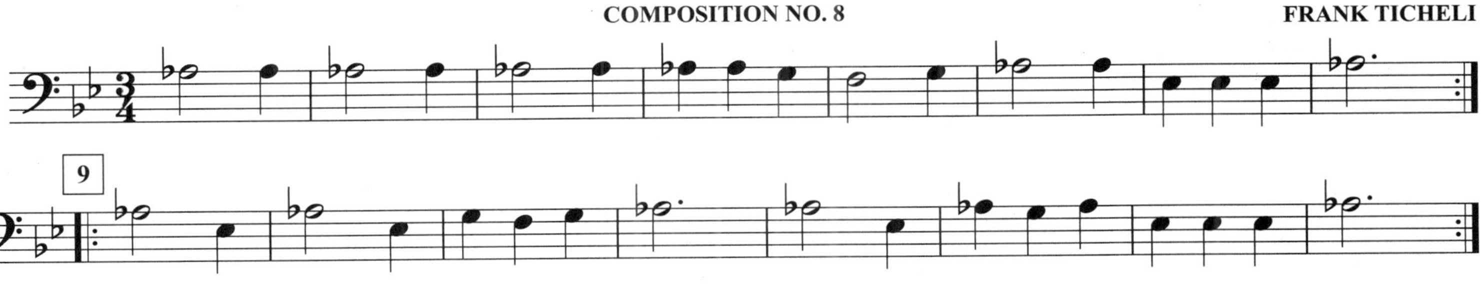

CREATIVE CORNER
No. 1 - Question & Answer

As a way of teaching creativity to one of his students, Mozart said jokingly to her:
"Look here, I've started this melody and can not finish it! Would you please finish it for me?"

Let's pretend you are Mozart's student!

You are given two fragments of a melody (the "Questions"). Provide the missing parts (the "Answers").

Here's how:

1. Perform the example below on your instrument. For the empty bars, count aloud the rhythms that are provided above the staff.
2. When ready, try improvising your own answers using the rhythms provided above the staff and only using notes in concert B♭ Major.
3. Finally, write down your own notes (perhaps one of your improvisations?) to fill in the blank bars. Then play through your finished melody!

Hints:

1. End on concert B♭ if you want your melody to sound complete. End on another note if you want it to sound as though it should go on.
2. Using mostly stepwise motion (e.g. F up to G, or D down to C, etc.) will help keep the melody smooth and flowing; an occasional leap (e.g., D up to G, or F down to D, etc.) is okay too!

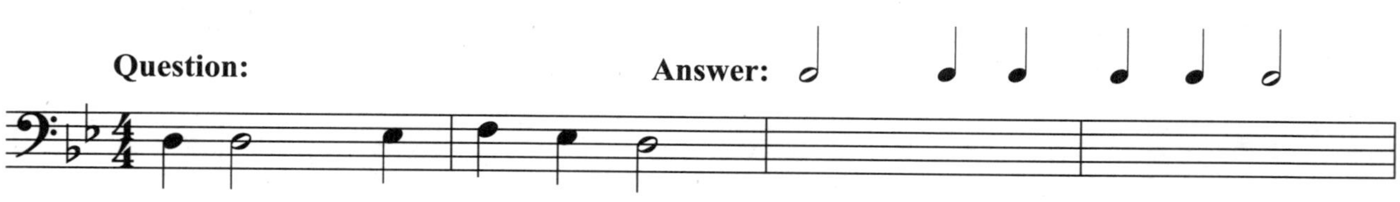

Daily Warmups & Drills

A set of fundamentals and exercises to improve sound, flexibility, articulation, and technique.

LONG TONES

Remember: Big breath, Shoulders down, Hold it steady, and Hold it out.

FLEXIBILITY

Remember: Connect all the notes with one breath, no space in between!

FOR ALL EXERCISES BELOW

Remember: Clear "T" syllable on every note. Practice slowly at first, then faster, then even ***FASTER!***

ARTICULATION

TECHNIQUE

TECHNIQUE

Practice these exercises for 5 minutes every day!

A little progress every day will greatly improve your playing!

LESSON 9

New in this lesson:

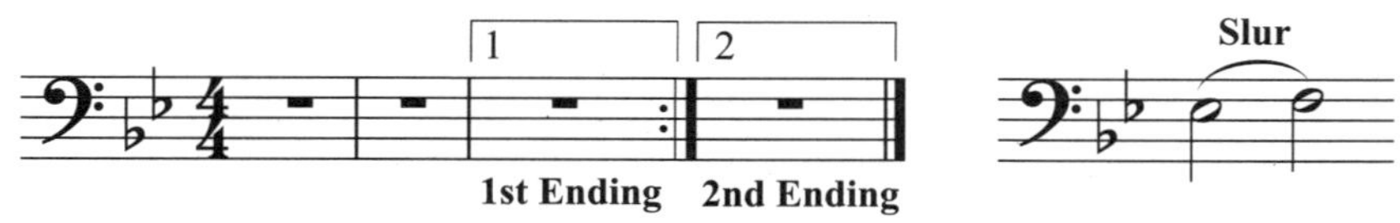

1

First & Second Endings

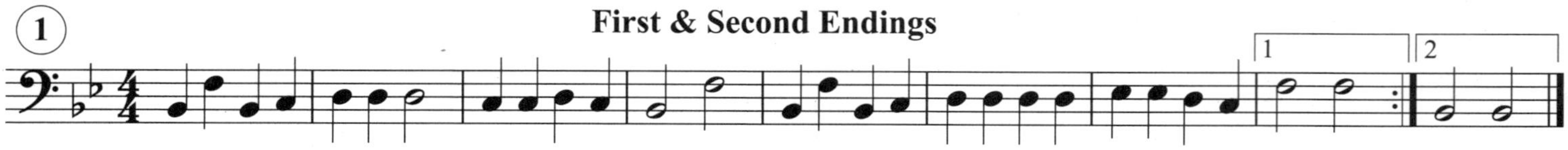

2

Roundabout

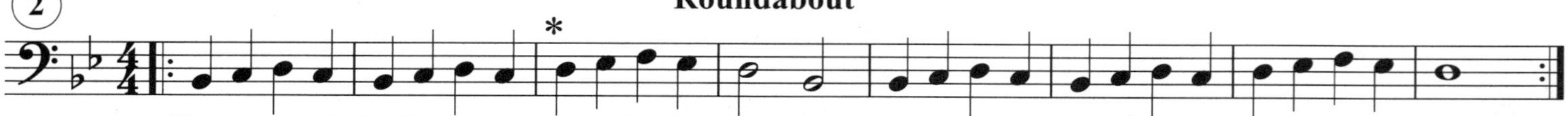

Play as a round! 1st Group start at beginning, 2nd Group wait and start when group 1 gets to measure 3 (*)

3

Slurring Half Notes

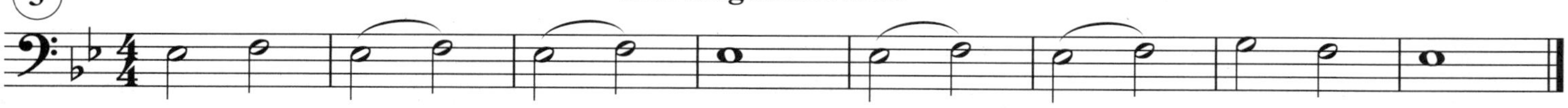

4

Slurring Quarter Notes

5

Crossing the Desert

March in the Minor Mode

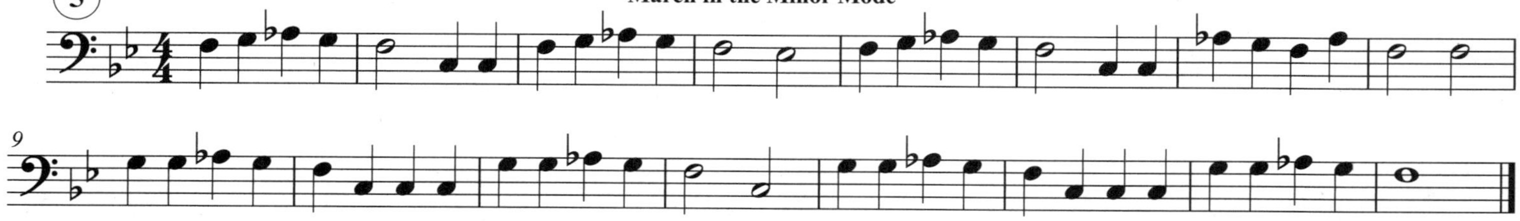

6

Counting Duet

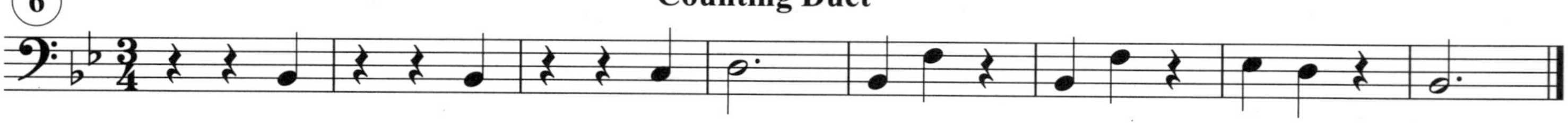

SACRED WATERS

COMPOSITION NO. 9

FRANK TICHELI

LESSON 10

New in this lesson:

Pickup Note — Accidental (Natural) — Four Note Slur — Multi-Bar Rest — E-Natural

(1) **Pickup Note**

(2) **Counting Measure Rests**

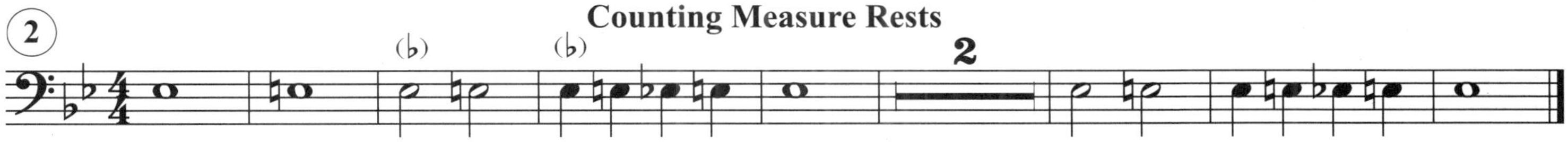

(3) **Four Notes Slurs**

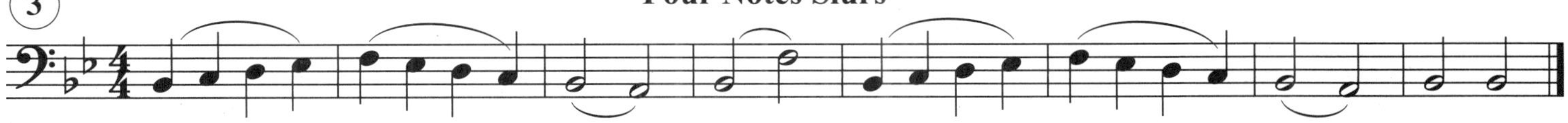

(4) **Accidentals**

(5) **A Waltz For Grampa**

(6) **Sad Walk**

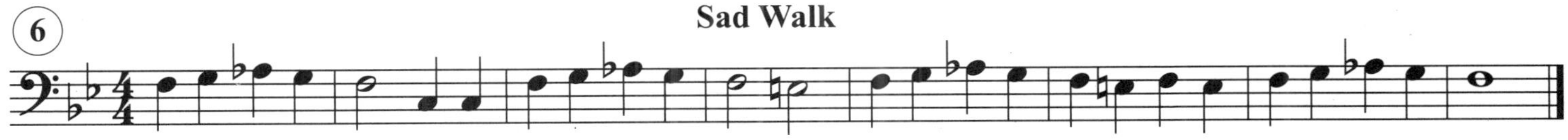

BIG OL' BEAR

COMPOSITION NO. 10

FRANK TICHELI

LESSON 11

New in this lesson:

NEW Key Signature
Concert E♭ Major

New Flat

1

Concert E♭ Major

2

3

4

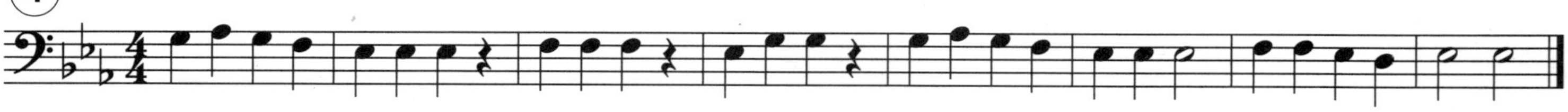

5

Jonathan Vanderpool

HYMN FOR JOSHUA

COMPOSITION NO. 11

FRANK TICHELI

LESSON 12

New in this lesson:

Da Capo al Fine

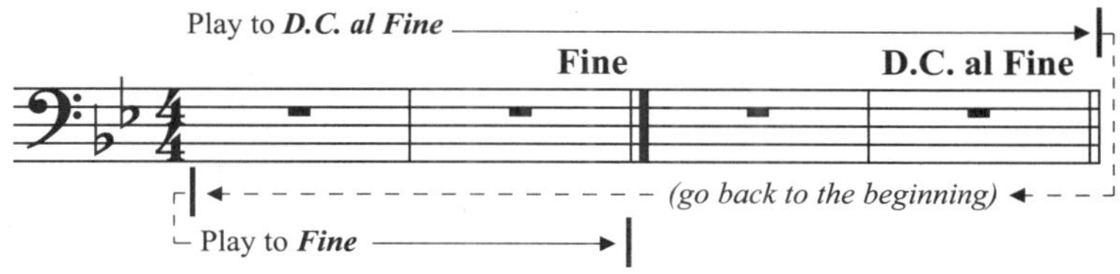

1 **Marching Home**

2

3

4 **Ode to Joy**

Ludwig van Beethoven

A WALK IN THE WOODS

COMPOSITION NO. 12

FRANK TICHELI

LESSON 13

New in this lesson:

EIGHTH NOTES

Two Eighth Notes
beamed together

Four Eighth Notes
beamed together

1 Eighth Notes

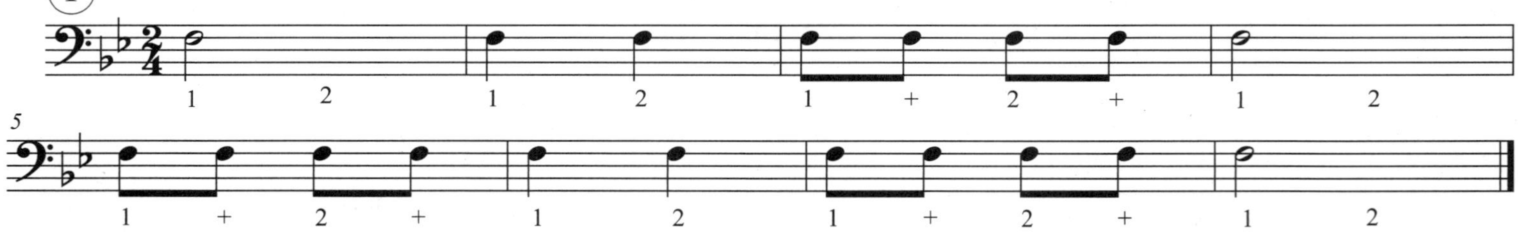

2

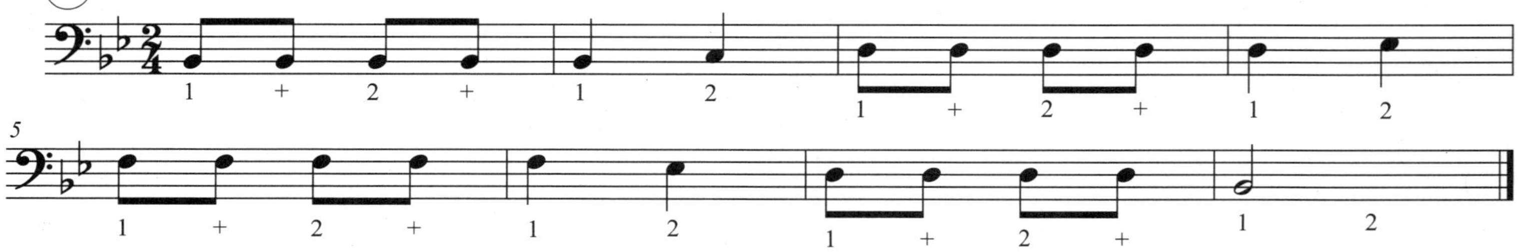

3 Quarter & Two Eighths Rhythm

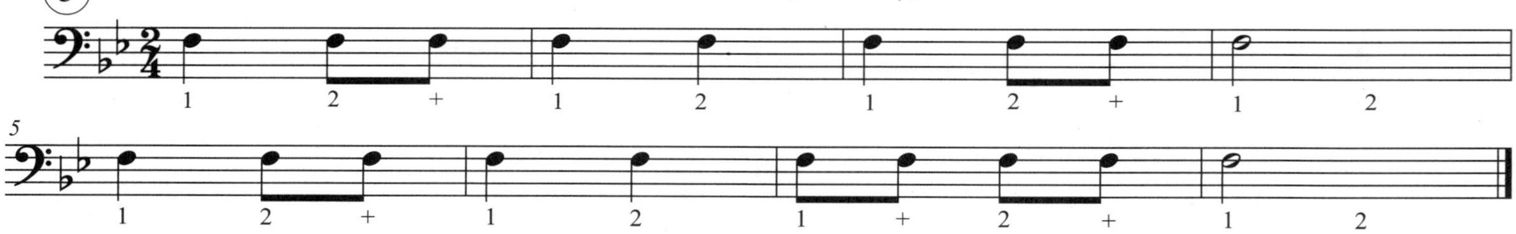

4 Two Eighths & Quarter Rhythm

5 Mississippi Mud Pie

6

Look At Me!

7

A SHORT RIDE ON HORSEBACK

COMPOSITION NO. 13

FRANK TICHELI

At a brisk trot

EUPHONIUM B.C.

LESSON 14

New in this lesson:

NEW Key Signature
Concert F Major

DYNAMICS
piano *(softly)* **forte** *(loudly)*

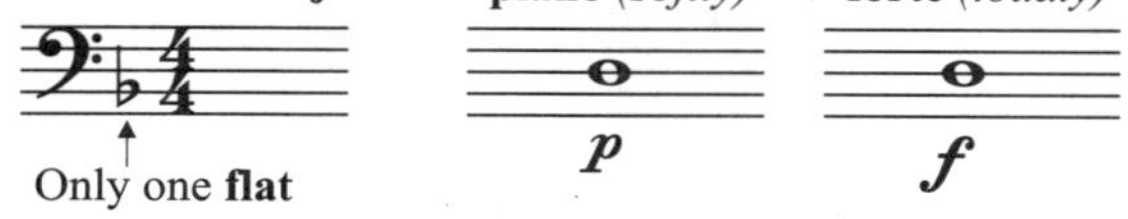

(1)

(2)

Skip To My Lou
(Fly's In The Buttermilk!)

Traditional

(3)

Concert F Major

(4)

(5)

(6)

American Song

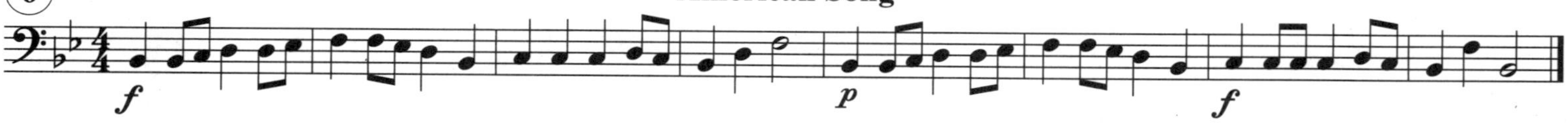

(7)

Same Song, New Key

A POLTERGEIST IN THE ATTIC
COMPOSITION NO. 14

FRANK TICHELI

Misterioso

Fine

9

D.C. al Fine

LESSON 15

New in this lesson:

Eighth Rests

1 Interval Study

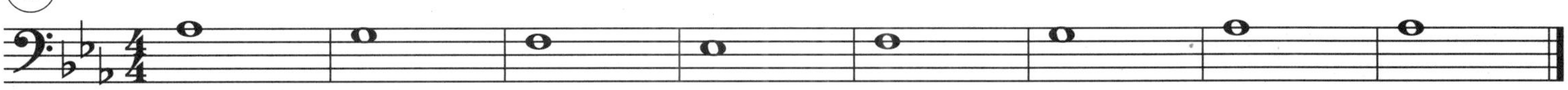

2 Chorale

3 Eighth Rests

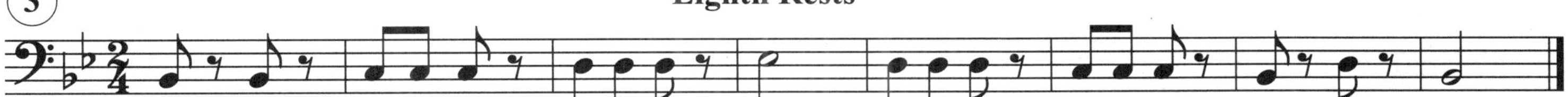

4

5 Da Capo Waltz

with *forte* and *piano*

6 Rain, Rain, Go Away

A song to play everyday it rains

Traditional

BRIGHT LIGHTS

COMPOSITION NO. 15

FRANK TICHELI

LESSON 16

New in this lesson:

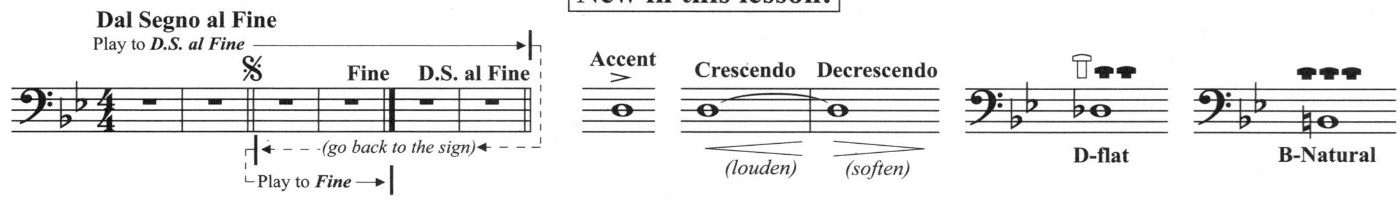

1 **Crescendo & Diminuendo**

2

3 **March To Victory**

4 **Little Waltz With Accents!**

5 **A Ghostly Walk**

6 **C Minor March**

AMAZING GRACE

COMPOSITION NO. 16

FRANK TICHELI

Flowing

CREATIVE CORNER
No. 2 - Words & Rhythm

The earliest documented music was all written for the voice, and musical rhythm evolved from the natural rhythms of spoken words.

Below is an example of a rhythmic setting of some words. Notice how the natural rhythm of the words is represented.

Example:

Your rhythmic setting:

Now it's your turn! Say the following words out loud several times. After you have said it enough times, and have memorized the rhythm, write down the rhythm in the staff above the words.

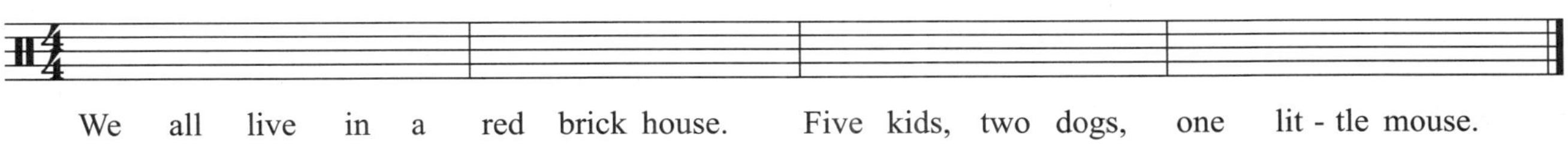

Advanced:

Make up your own words (16 syllables or less), and write them below the staff below, then set them to your own rhythms. Try to reflect the natural rhythms of the words!

EUPHONIUM B.C.

Intermediate Daily Warmups & Drills

A set of fundamentals and exercises to improve sound, flexibility, articulation, and technique.

LONG TONES

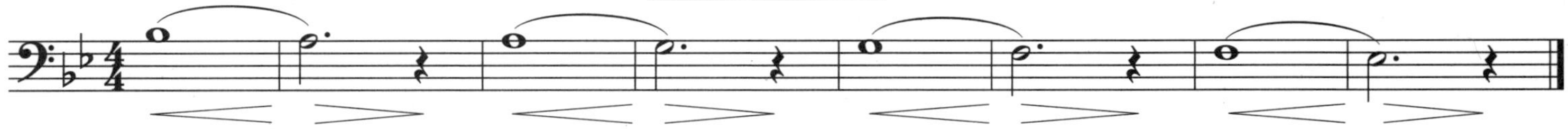

LIP SLURS

Practice open, and then lower with second valve, and then first valve.

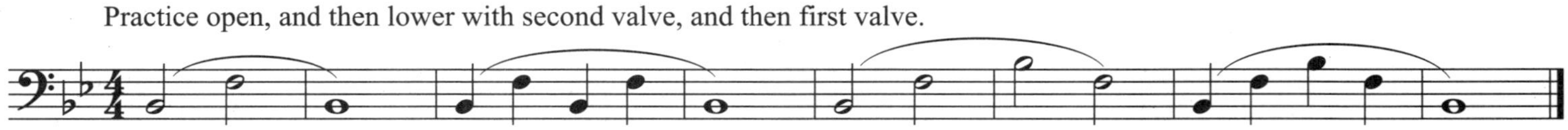

FOR ALL EXERCISES BELOW

Remember: Clear "T" syllable on every note. Practice slowly at first, then faster, then even ***FASTER!***

ARTICULATION

TECHNIQUE

TECHNIQUE

Practice these exercises for 5 minutes every day!

A little progress every day will greatly improve your playing!

LESSON 17

New in this lesson:

Staccato Markings (Dots) → Plays the same as this

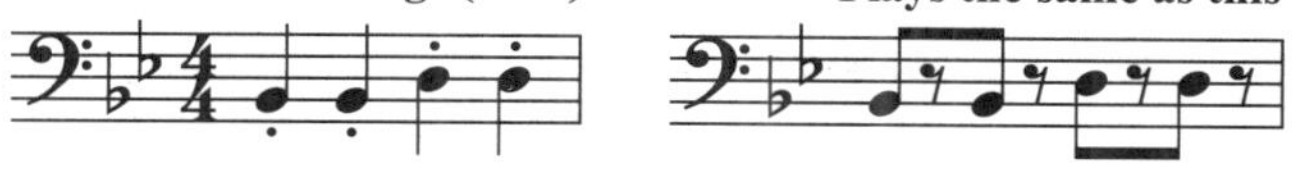

(1)

Play these measures the same as the first four measures.

(2)

(3)

(4)

Staccato Counting Duet

(5)

Lightly Row

Traditional

CIRCUS MARCH

COMPOSITION NO. 17

FRANK TICHELI

March Tempo

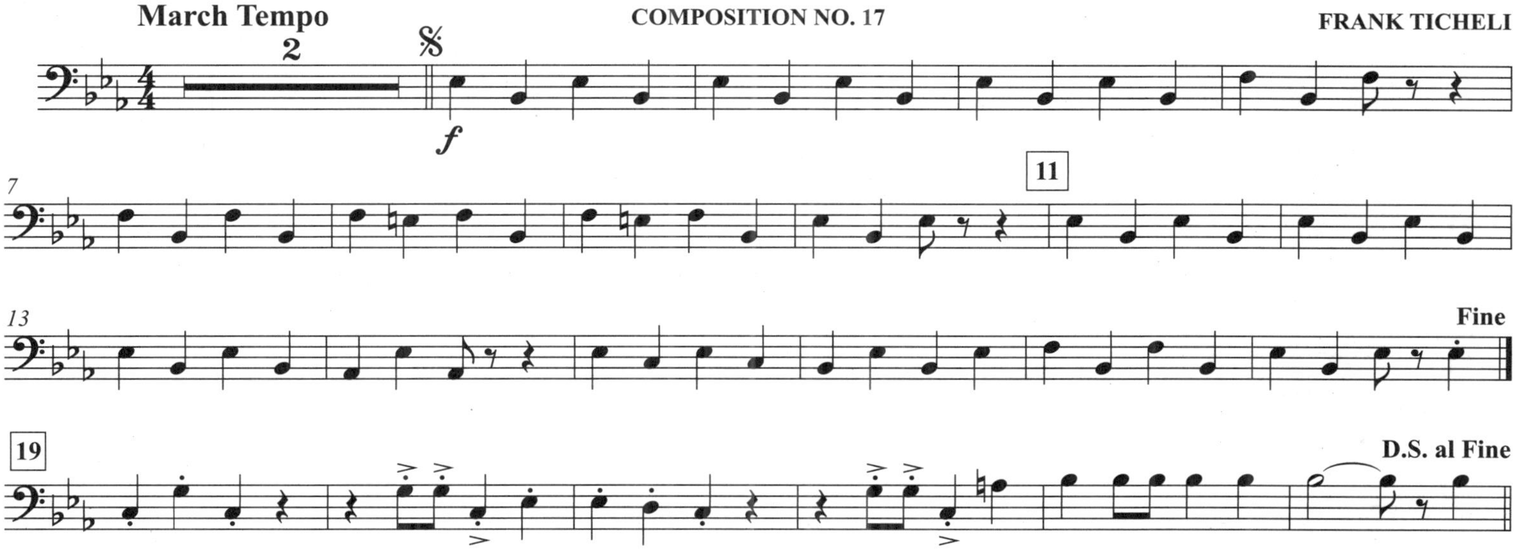

LESSON 18

New in this lesson:

NEW Key Signature
Concert A♭ Major

Slur Two - Tongue Two

mezzo-piano *(medium soft)*

mezzo-forte *(medium loud)*

legato marking

Tempo marking **Allegro**

1 Slur Two, Tongue Two

2 Concert A♭ Major

Rest Review

3 Oh, When The Saints

Allegro

Traditional

4 Rustic Song

Smooth and Connected

A PEACEFUL MOMENT

COMPOSITION NO. 18

FRANK TICHELI

Legato

LESSON 19

New in this lesson:

NEW Rhythm

Dotted Quarter Note
followed by **Eighth Note**

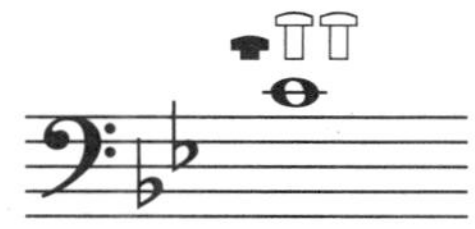

(1)

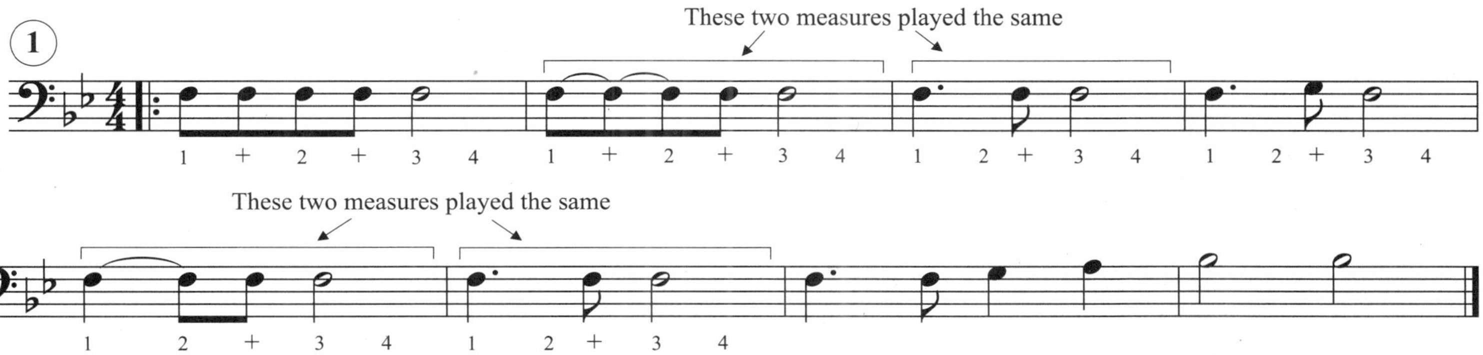

(2)

Dotted Quarter & Eighth

(3)

America

Traditional

(4)

High Note Practice

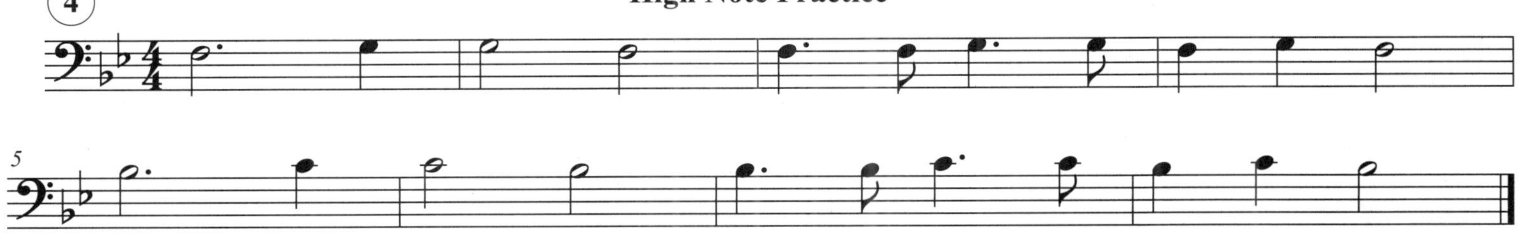

Alouette

5 **Moderato**

Traditional

A French Round

6 **Andante**

Traditional

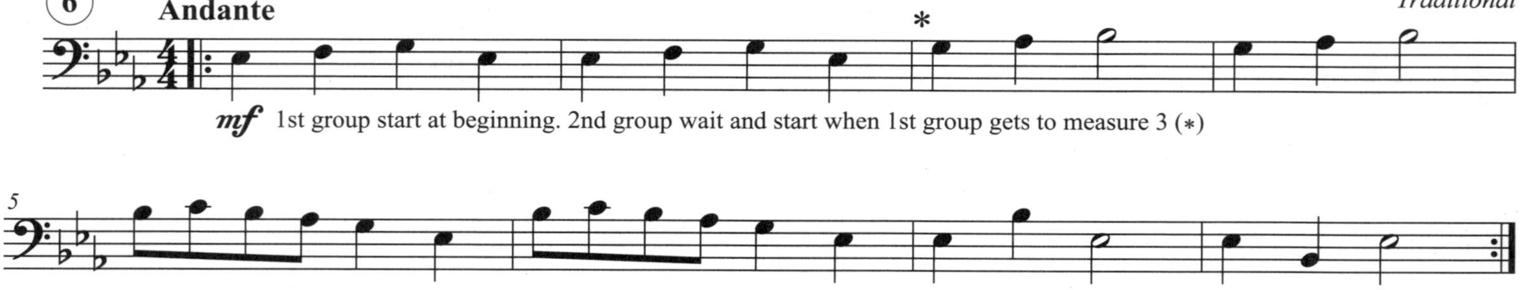

SONG FOR HANNAH

COMPOSITION NO. 19

FRANK TICHELI

Majestic

LESSON 20

New in this lesson:

Eighth Note Combinations Review
Fermata

Eighth Note Rhythm Review

1

Camptown Races

2 **Allegro**

Stephen Foster

3

A Theme from Symphony No. 3 (Eroica)

Ludwig van Beethoven

4

VARIATION ON A THEME BY BEETHOVEN

COMPOSITION NO. 20

FRANK TICHELI

Allegro

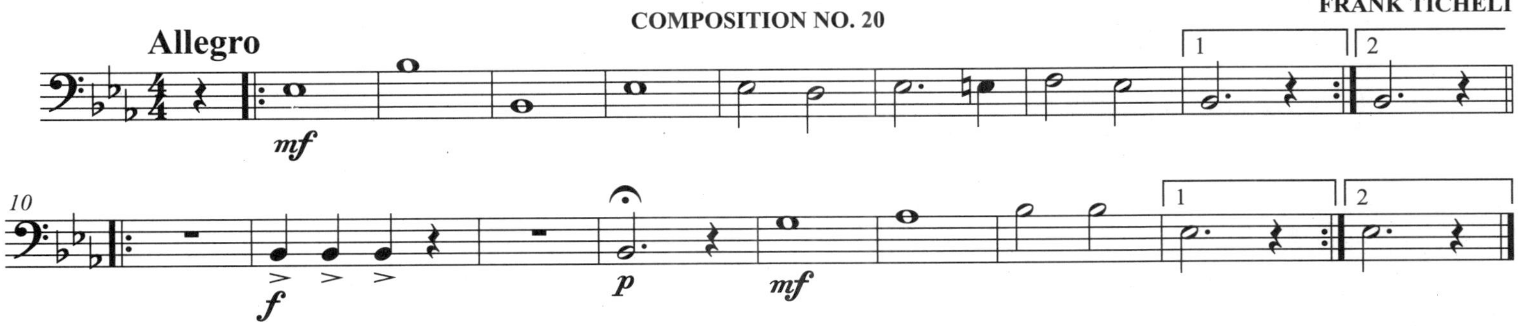

LESSON 21

New in this lesson:

Slurs Over Bar Line

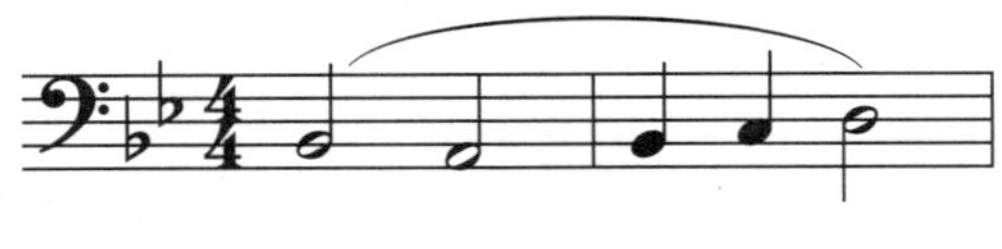

1 **Two-Measure Slurs**

2 **Dotted Quarter Master March**

3 **Beats & After-Beats**

4 **Yankee Doodle**

Traditional

Allegro

FUNERAL MARCH

COMPOSITION NO. 21

FRANK TICHELI

Andante Moderato

LESSON 22

A trip to the British Isles

New in this lesson:

NEW Rhythm

Eighth Note followed by **Dotted Quarter Note**

Irish Reel

1 **Moderato** *Traditional*

Shepherd's Hey

2 **Moderato** *Traditional*

Sweet Molly Malone

3 **Andante** *Traditional*

SPRING BURSTS OUT

COMPOSITION NO. 22

FRANK TICHELI

Allegro Molto

CREATIVE CORNER

No. 3 - "All The World's A Stage"

for performers using only their bodies as instruments

by Frank Ticheli

Performance Instructions:

1. Divide any number of performers into three groups (Group A, B, and C).
2. Each group follows the instructions provided in their assigned column (A, B, or C).
3. All performers begin at the top of their respective column (Section 1).
4. When conductor holds up two fingers, each group moves down to section 2 immediately.
5. *Option*: The conductor may wish to cue groups independently. For example, Group A may be cued to move on to Section 2 before Groups B and C, *etc*.

	GROUP A	GROUP B	GROUP C
Section 1	Click tongue quietly about once every two seconds. Do not increase speed or volume.	Whistle any pitch *quietly.* You may whistle a made-up tune, a random pitch, or glissando between pitches.	Slap hands on lap at random and varied speed.
Section 2	Remain silent.	Loudly whisper the following letters, in short bursts of sound: P K T …in any order with one or two seconds of silence between each letter.	Make the sound, "*Shhh…*" for as long as one breath will allow.
Section 3 *(Gets louder and louder!)*	Stomp feet on ground quietly at first; gradually increase speed and volume!	Click tongue quietly about once every two seconds at first; gradually click tongue louder, more rapidly!	Cough quietly once every two seconds at first; gradually increase frequency and volume of coughing!
Section 4	Snap fingers of both hands at rapid speed; gradually fade to silence.	Imitate the sound of a gentle breeze blowing through the trees. Fade to silence.	Whisper (*unvoiced*) the words below from Shakespeare, slowly and in any order: *"All the world's a stage, and all the men and women merely players."*

Discussion:

1. What did you like about the piece? What did you dislike? Why?
2. The work reaches a climax in Section 3, then slowly dies away in Section 4. Discuss this. Is the form satisfying? Why or why not?
3. Could you make changes to improve the composition or your performance of it? For example, could you change dynamics, cut sections, re-order sections, perform it backwards?

Now It's Your Turn!

Compose your own "alternative piece," placing written instructions in the grid below. Sounds could be limited to only those that can be produced by the human voice or body, or may be expanded to include sounds made by pots and pans, cups and glasses, coins, sheets of paper, clay pots, salad bowls, or any other "found" objects. Have fun!

	GROUP A	GROUP B	GROUP C
Section 1			
Section 2			
Section 3			
Section 4			

LESSON 23

New in this lesson:

NEW Rhythm | **Change of Time Signature** | **Maestoso**

Eighth Note in simple syncopation

1

These two measures played the same

2

Syncopation

3

Syncopation With Accents

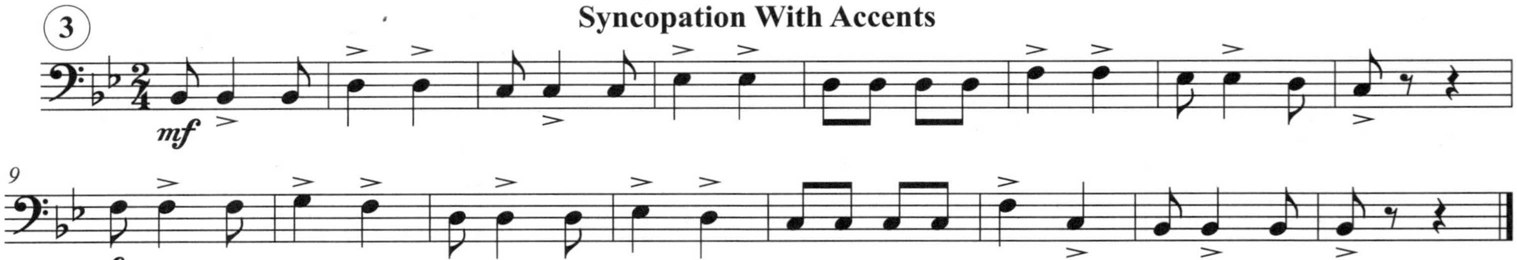

4 **Maestoso**

The Old Country

DANCING ON AIR

COMPOSITION NO. 23

FRANK TICHELI

Allegro

LESSON 24

New in this lesson:

REVIEW

1 **Allegro**

2 **Andante**

3 **Maestoso**

4 **Moderato**

5 **Andante**

RUSSIAN DANCE

COMPOSITION NO. 24

FRANK TICHELI

Allegro Molto

SCALES & ARPEGGIOS

Practice *all* scales that have been assigned to you everytime you practice.
Practice old scales for review and new scales as they are added.

Concert B♭ Major

B♭ Scale

Concert E♭ Major

E♭ Scale

Concert A♭ Major

A♭ Scale

Concert F Major

F Scale

SUNDAY MORNING

FOR SOLO EUPHONIUM B.C.
With or Without Piano

Solo Euphonium Part

FRANK TICHELI

SUNDAY MORNING, for Solo Euphonium
We end Book I of *Making Music Matter* with a solo piece for your instrument! This piece may be performed with or without piano. (The piano accompaniment is on the next pages.)

This solo piece is provided as a reward for all of your accomplishments. You could play this piece for family or friends, or in a public recital. Or you could just have fun playing the piece for your own personal enjoyment.

About this Solo Piece

The euphonium has an expressive sound that reminds me of the human voice. The instrument sings! I tried to bring out this trait in *Sunday Morning.* As the title suggests, the piece also has a kind of reverent quality about it, like a church congregation singing out in full voices.

- Pay attention to the accented eighth-notes in measure 6 and 30, and be sure to bring them out (with the piano). These accents provide dynamic contrast, and give a sense of purpose to the melody.

- Notice that bars 9 to 16 contain an almost an exact repeat of the first eight bars, with one notable exception—the first eight bars are marked ***f*** whereas the next eight are marked ***mp***. I imagine the second phrase as an echo to the first. Be sure to bring out this dynamic contrast.

- Starting at bar 17, the euphonium and piano engage in a little question and answer game. Rhythmic accuracy is essential here.

- The quarter-notes in bars 17, 18, 21, and 22 are marked as *staccato.* Remember that *staccato* notes, while shorter than unmarked notes, should still have some length. Think "tuh" rather than "tut" so that you don't clip the release in an unmusical way.

EUPHONIUM B.C.

SUNDAY MORNING

FOR SOLO EUPHONIUM B.C.
With or Without Piano

Piano Score

Allegro Moderato ♩ = c. 126

FRANK TICHELI

The original owner of this book is licensed to photocopy this and the next page for purposes of practice and performance.

16
17
mf
21
cresc.
cresc.
25
f
mf
29
rit.

GLOSSARY OF TERMS

ABA Form. ABA refers to the structure of a composition. There are three parts—an "A" part, a "B" part, and another "A" part. When you hear a piece that begins and ends with the same melody (the "A" part) but has a different melody in between (the "B" part), you are hearing a work in ABA Form.

Accent. (>) The accent always appears over or under the notehead, and can appear at any dynamic level (loudness level). When you see this mark, you should play the beginning of the note more strongly.

Accidental. Accidentals change the pitch of a note; they occur in the course of a piece. In the music in this book, you will see three kinds of accidentals: the flat sign (♭), the natural sign (♮), and the sharp sign (♯). One important rule: *an accidental has effect only in the same measure in which it appears, and only in the octave in which it appears.*

Allegro. Italian for "cheerful." Tempo indication to play at a lively, brisk, rapid speed. Pronunciation: *ah-LEH-groh*

Andante. Italian for "going," "moving," "walking;" Tempo indication to play at a moderate, easily flowing pace. Pronunciation: *ahn-DAHN-tay*

Articulation. Refers to the way in which a note is begun, since the beginning of a note (also referred to as the note's "attack") changes its sound in many ways. Mastery over articulation is one of the most important ways in which you can make your playing expressive. The range of expression is nearly infinite.

Bar Line. This is the thin vertical line drawn through the staff to mark the end of each bar or measure. (The words *bar* and *measure* mean the same thing.)

Clef (Treble Clef: 𝄞; Bass Clef: 𝄢 Percussion Clef: 𝄥). The purpose of a clef—any clef—is to mark the location on the staff of a particular pitch. The Treble Clef circles around the second line of the staff (the "G" above "middle C")—thus it's also called the "G Clef." The Bass Clef has two dots that surround the fourth line of the staff to mark the "F" below "middle C"—thus it's also called the "F Clef." The percussion clef indicates that the instrument has no definite pitch; for example, a snare drum has no definite pitch.

Common Time. 𝄴 An alternative manner to indicate 4/4 time signature.

Crescendo. Italian for "Growing," increasing in loudness, indicated either by the symbol: 𝆒, or by the abbreviation, *cresc*. Pronunciation: *kreh-SHEHN-doh*

D.C. al Fine. "From the beginning to the end;" go back to the beginning and play to the bar marked "Fine." (*D.C.* is an abbreviation for the Italian, *Da Capo,* which means "to the head" – and *al Fine* is Italian for "to the end". Pronunciation: *Dah-CAH-poh ahl-FEE-nay*

D.S. al Fine. "From the sign to the end"; go back to the sign 𝄋 and play to the bar marked "*fine*." (*D.S.,* is the abbreviation for the Italian, *Dal Segno,* which means "to the sign". Pronunciation: *Dahl-SEHN-yo*)

Decrescendo (or, Diminuendo). Italian for decreasing in loudness, either indicated by the symbol: ——— or by the abbreviation *decresc.* or the abbreviation *dim.* (for *diminuendo*). Pronunciations: *Day-kreh-SHEHN-do; dih-mihn-yoo-EHN-do.*

Diatonic. Relating to the notes in a given key. For example, in the key of B♭ Major, the diatonic notes would be B♭, C, D, E♭, F, G, A.

Divisi. Italian for "Divided." Signifies that two parts are written on one staff, with one or more players of the same instrument playing each part. Pronunciation: *dee-VEE-see*

Dotted Half-Note. 𝅗𝅥. A half-note with a dot placed after it, increasing its value by one-half (for example, in 4/4 time, a dotted half-note has the value of three beats).

Dotted Quarter-Note. ♩. A quarter-note with a dot placed after it, increasing its value by one-half (for example, in 4/4 time, a dotted quarter-note has the value of one and a half beats).

Eighth-Note. ♪ A note indicated with a flag or single beam, receiving half the value of a quarter note (for example, in 4/4 time there are two eighth-notes in one beat, and eight eighth-notes in one bar).

Eighth-Note Rest. 𝄾 indicating a rest for the duration of one eighth-note.

Fermata. 𝄐 Italian for "Held". Pronunciation: *fehr-MAH-tah.*

Flat Sign. [♭] Indication for a note to be lowered by a semitone, or one-half step (for example, E lowered to E-flat).

Forte. Italian for "Strong," "loud"; in music, indicated as ***f*** as an instruction for the player to play loudly. Pronunciation: *FOR-tay*

Four Quarter Time. 4/4; also referred to as "Common Time", time signature found at the beginning of a piece to indicate four beats in each bar, with the quarter-note receiving the beat.

Half-Note. 𝅗𝅥 A note that receives twice the value of a quarter-note (for example, in 4/4 time, a half-note receives two beats).

Half-Rote Rest. 𝄼 indicating a rest for the duration of one half-note.

Hymn. A religious or sacred song or piece, usually intended to be sung by a church congregation; in instrumental music, a songlike piece religious or devotional in character.

Key Signature. The sharps or flats indicated at the beginning of each staff to indicate the "key" of a composition. The word "key" refers to the note around which a composition gravitates (centers). For example, in B♭ Major, the composition centers around the note B-flat.

Legato. Italian for "Tied together"; indication for notes to be tongued smoothly, in a connected way, with little or no silence between the notes. See also: *staccato*. Pronunciation: *Leh-GAH-toh*

Maestoso. Italian for "Majestic, dignified." To play in a lofty, dignified, or majestic style. Pronunciation: *My-STOH-soh*

Marcato. Italian for "Marked"; played with distinctness and emphasis. Pronunciation: *mahr-CAH-toh*

March. A composition with either 2 or 2 beats in a measure, generally in 2/4, 2/2, 4/4, or 6/8 time, with steady beat, and intended to musically represent marching.

Mezzo Piano. Italian for moderately soft; indicated as ***mp*** as an instruction for the player to play at a moderately soft volume. Pronunciation: *MET-soh pee-AH-noh*

Moderato. Italian for "Moderate;" tempo indication to play at a moderate pace, neither very fast nor very slow. Pronunciation: *moh-deh-RAH-toh*

Multiple Measure Rest. 

An indication for the player to rest for a specified number of bars (for example, in this case, three bars). Also known as "Block Rest" or "Extended Rest."

Natural Sign. [♮] Indication for a note to be played at its normal pitch; usually used to cancel a flat or sharp.

Octave. When you learn two notes that have the same letter name, for example, Low C and High C, these notes are said to be one octave apart. An octave is a span (distance) of eight diatonic notes.

Piano. Italian for "soft." Indicated as ***p*** as an instruction for the player to play softly. Pronunciation: *pee-AH-noh*

Pickup Note. Also referred to as an "Upbeat" or "Anacrusis"; one or more notes at the beginning of a melody that occur before the first bar line.

Quarter-Note. ♩ A note that receives one-quarter the value of a whole-note (for example, in 4/4 time, a quarter-note receives one beat).

Quarter-Note Rest. 𝄽 indicating a rest for the duration of one quarter-note.

Renaissance. In music, representing the period of ca. 1430-1650; music of this period is wide ranging in style, and is often divided into "sacred" (of the church) and "secular" (non-church related) types.

Rit. Abbreviation for the Italian, *Ritardando*. Gradually decrease the tempo. Pronunciation: *ree-tahr-DAHN-do*

Round. A composition in which voices or instruments play a given melody in succession, one after the other, rather than together. (A good example of a round is "Row, Row, Row your Boat.")

Scale. A series of tones that form a major or minor scale, or chromatic scale (all 12 tones within an octave), or any series of tones that occur within an octave.

Sharp Sign. [♯] Indication for a note to be raised by a semitone, or one-half step (for example, F raised to F-sharp)

Sixteenth-Note. 𝅘𝅥𝅯 A note receiving one quarter the value of a quarter-note (for example, in 4/4 time there are four sixteenth-notes in one beat, and sixteen sixteenth-notes in one bar).

Slur. A curved line  signifying that the notes are to be played in *legato* fashion without being tongued. When notes appear under a slur, only the first note is tongued; the others are to be played on one breath without being tongued.

Staccato. ♩ for "Detached, separated;" a style in which the notes are separated from one another. See also: *legato*.
Pronunciation: *stah-KAH-toh*

Staff. The five parallel lines upon which music is notated. You will always find a clef at the start of each staff. See also: *Clef*.

Syncopation. Any rhythm that contradicts the normal pulse of meter and rhythm. For example,  indicate in 4/4.

Three Quarter Time. 3/4; a time signature shown at the beginning of a piece to indicate three beats in each bar, with the quarter-note receiving the beat.

Tempo. The speed at which a piece of music is to be played, often indicated by a *metronome* marking. For example, ♩ = 100 indicates a fast tempo in which there are 100 quarter-notes per minute. A moderate tempo would be ♩ = 80 and a slow tempo would be ♩ = 60 At that tempo, each beat is one second long.

Tie. A curved line  joining two notes of the same pitch together as one (for example two tied quarter-notes are played the same as a half-note).

Time Signature. An indication at the beginning of a piece shown as two numbers, one above the other. The the upper number indicates the number of beats in the bar, and the lower number indicates what kind of note receives one beat. For example, a time signature of 3/4 indicates that there are three beats in a bar, and that the quarter-note receives one beat.

Two Quarter Time. 2/4; a time signature shown at the beginning of a piece to indicate two beats in each bar, with the quarter-note receiving the beat.

Unison. The performance of a single melody by two or more players, either at exactly the same pitch or in different octaves; in music, the term is often used to cancel a *divisi* indication.

Waltz. A dance in 3/4 time, which can be in any tempo from slow to moderately fast.

Whole-Note. 𝅝 A note that receives twice the value of a half-note (for example, in 4/4 time, a whole-note receives four beats).

Whole-Note Rest.  indicating a rest for the duration of one whole-note.

PRESERVING OUR MUSIC

IT IS IMPORTANT TO PRESERVE OUR MUSICAL HERITAGE
FOR FUTURE GENERATIONS

Acidic paper has been in widespread use since the turn of the century, and has become the bane of archivists, librarians, and others who seek to preserve knowledge intact, because it literally will self-destruct as it ages. Some paper, only three or four decades old, already has become impossible to handle — so brittle it crumbles to the touch. Surely we do not want today's music to be unavailable to those who will inhabit the future. If the music of the Renaissance had not been written on vellum it could never have been preserved and we would not have it today, some four hundred years later. Let us give the same consideration to the musicians in our future.

It was with this thinking that Manhattan Beach Music in 1988 first addressed the needs of the archivist by printing all of its concert band music on acid-free paper that met the standards specified in the American National Standard for Information Sciences — Permanence of Paper for Printed Library Materials (ANSI Z39.48-1984). The standard was revised on October 26, 1992 to include coated papers; all of our new editions and reprints of older editions meet this revised standard. With proper care and under proper environmental conditions, this paper should last for at least several hundred years.

Technical notes: Paper permanence is related to several factors: The acidity or alkalinity (pH) of the paper is perhaps the most critical criterion. Archival paper (also known as acid-free paper, alkaline paper, and permanent paper) is acid-free, has a pH between 7.5 and 10, is tear resistant, has an alkaline reserve equivalent to 2% calcium carbonate (to neutralize any acid that might arise from natural aging of the paper or from environmental pollution), and contains no unbleached pulp or groundwood (no more than 1% lignin by weight). The specific standards summarized here are set forth in detail by the National Information Standards Organization in American National Standard Z39.48-1992. For more information, contact: NISO, 4733 Bethesda Avenue, Suite 300, Bethesda, MD 20814, http://www.niso.org/

This paper meets the requirements of ANSI/NISO Z39.48-1992
(Permanence of Paper) ∞

MANHATTAN BEACH MUSIC
BOB MARGOLIS — NEIL RUDDY
PUBLISHERS AND COFOUNDERS

PRINTING: CHERNAY PRINTING, INC.